History for Kids: The Mongol Empire

Contents

Introduction

There was a time when mere mention of the mighty Mongols inspired fear in those who had heard the stories and commanded respect in those who had met them in the field. It certainly is a strange twist of history that present-day Mongolia is such a peaceful place that is barely ever mentioned on the news. Without knowing their history, one would probably never imagine that the Mongols were once the most fearsome warriors who took the world by storm and built one of the largest empires in the history of civilization.

Indeed, people consider the Mongol Empire to be the largest contiguous empire in history, meaning that it was the largest one to have been entirely connected by land. The Mongol Empire is second to the British Empire when it comes to the total land area they controlled, but the Mongol realm was the biggest empire where a person could walk from one end to the other.

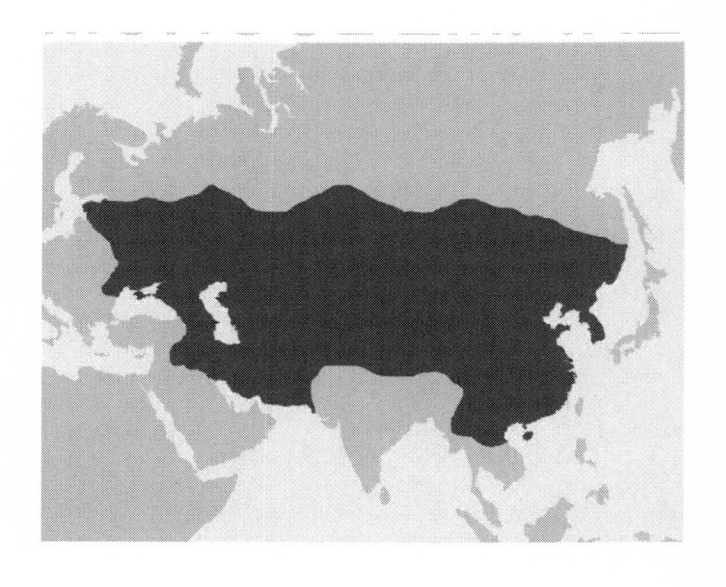

Map of the Mongol Empire

The rise of the Mongols also came as something of a shock to the world not just because of their rapid conquests but also the locale and the circumstances from which they arose. The Mongols used to be little more than nomads prowling the harsh and often barren steppes of Mongolia. These environments were certainly not ideal, especially when compared to other locations where civilizations flourished through the millennia. Adversity usually gives birth to strength, however, and the Mongols are a fine example of this principle in practice. Without nature's blessing and with the odds often stacked against them, the Mongols brought the world to heel nonetheless.

Rising to prominence in the early 13th century, the Mongols built their empire after a process of unification between many tribes throughout Mongolia and elsewhere in northeastern Asia under one unifier, who became the Great Khan. This first Great Khan was the (in) famous Genghis Khan, one of the most fearsome and prolific war leaders who shook the world.

The statue of Genghis Khan at the Government Palace in Ulan Bator, Mongolia

Among other things, the Mongols owed their successes to their military tactics and impressive art of war, which relied heavily on incredible horsemanship, archery, and other fighting skills.

After all, the steppes were most likely the kind of environment where the horse was first domesticated, so the Mongols and their ancestors had been using them for thousands of years.

Mongolian shepherd on horseback

Of course, as we now know, the Mongolian military successes weren't owed solely to their adeptness at war. The Mongols were often ruthless and gave no quarter to their enemies. Perhaps in quite a contrast to some other aspects of their empire, the Mongols approached warfare with a merciless attitude, leading to the deaths of millions upon millions of people during their conquests. Certainly, such was life in the harsh times of the old days, but the Mongols took things to a whole new level. Resisting and refusing to submit to the whim of the incoming Mongols could often mean extinction for entire nations.

The Mongol Empire was much more than just war and conquest, though. The Mongols accomplished many feats and altered the history of the world forever in more ways than one. In this book, we will explore the origins and many other particularities of this fascinating warrior people during their finest hours.

Chapter I:
The Mongols and Their Background

Officially, the Mongol Empire reigned between 1206 and 1368, which is the main period we will focus on throughout this book. However, as is always the case, there was plenty of history that predated these important events and paved the way for the era in question. In the course of that era, the Mongols went from being a number of nomadic steppe tribes to a unified force that would annex numerous other empires and cultures throughout Asia and beyond.

First and foremost, it's important to note that, historically and geographically speaking, "Mongolia" can refer to an area that stretches beyond the borders of the present-day Republic of the same name. The modern country is landlocked between Russia and China to the north and south, respectively. Today's Mongolia corresponds to what has historically been known as Outer Mongolia, while Inner Mongolia, just to the south, is still an autonomous region in China.

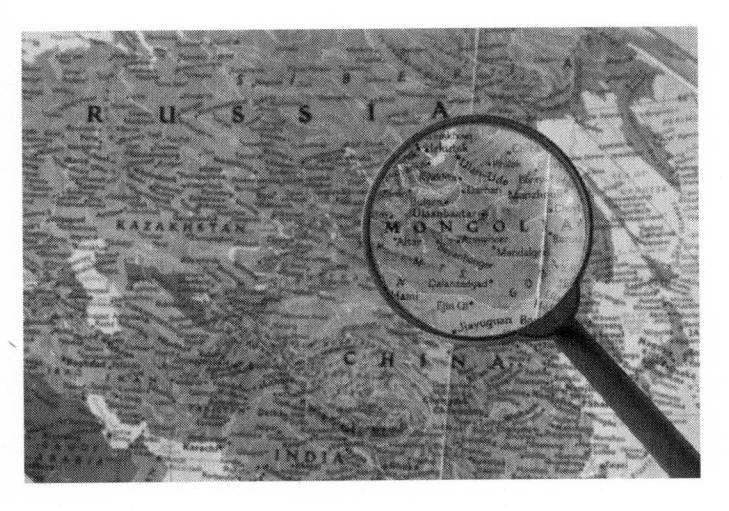

Map of Mongolia

Combined with a couple of smaller regions in Russia to the north, these lands can collectively be referred to as the Mongolian Plateau. Another important area is Manchuria, which is a region in present-day China just to the east of Inner Mongolia, north of the Korean Peninsula. Historically, these and other regions toward western China were ruled by rivaling Chinese dynasties, which formed a complex political situation. All the while, various nomadic tribes prowled the steppes to the north, often divided and engaged in intertribal conflict.

Mongol Origins

As you can imagine, many things about the exact origins of the Mongols are uncertain, and we don't know much about them prior to their rise in the 12th century. The most likely scenarios are that the early Mongols were either indigenous Asiatic people on the Mongolian Plateau or descendants of people who moved in from the Siberian steppes at some point.

Be that as it may, traces of human activity not just in Mongolia but all over the Eurasian steppes go back to the Paleolithic Period. During the Stone Age, more than 100,000 years ago, humans were already prowling the southern parts of Mongolia and the Gobi Desert. People continuously inhabited the area since then, and semblances of some early tribal formations began to appear roughly around the 1st millennium BC, although some of the important artifacts found in Outer Mongolia were significantly older. Going as far back as 5,000 years, artifacts, remains of settlements, and various structures such as tombs are throughout Mongolia.

Around 1500 BC, climate changes in this region had a large impact on how local populations developed. Mongolia became colder, and the climate grew increasingly dry, which affected the people's ability to maintain farms. This shift most likely led the nomads in Mongolia to focus on keeping livestock as the main source of food. Certainly, farming and agriculture were known to these people of the plains, but their conditions simply made livestock more viable.

As such, the Mongols and their ancestors are better viewed as herders instead of farmers, with the latter being the most common way of life in much of the known world at the time. Most importantly, the harsh conditions in the steppes made the Mongols tough as nails, and their way of life cultivated the development of certain skills that would later prove crucial for their success. For one, horsemanship was crucial to navigating the open plains, so the Mongols focused on becoming great horsemen. They also selectively bred their horses for speed and agility. On top of that, hunting in the steppes necessitated ranged weapons due to a lack of cover for sneaking and hiding. For this reason, the Mongols became such renowned archers.

According to Chinese historiography, the Mongols, or at least some of their precursor tribes, were initially located around the Ergune River, which is one of the rivers flowing along the present-day Russo-Chinese border. From this locale, the Mongols might have migrated westward into parts of present-day Mongolia in the 7th century, particularly around the rivers Onon, Kerulen, and Tuul.

Ergune River

What would later become the Mongols was probably a loose group of several tribes at that time. When referring to the Mongols as "Mengwu," the Chinese records from that time were talking about just one of the Mongolian tribes. Indeed, the Mongolian Plateau and areas further north, around the Lake Baikal in Russia, were occupied by numerous nomadic tribes, some of which are now well-known, such as the Tatars. Other tribes or, rather, confederations of tribes included the Khamag Mongols, Keraites, Merkits, and others.

Even though loosely related and often warring Mongol tribes were spread over the Mongolian Plateau since as early as 2,000 years BC, they wouldn't really dominate the region for quite a long time. Over the centuries, the Eurasian steppes saw the rise of various peoples like the Scythians, Xiongnu, ancient Turkic peoples, and the Uyghurs.

All in all, it's clear that the Eurasian steppes and the Mongolian Plateau itself was teeming with human activity for millennia. The people who would later be known as the Mongols were merely a drop in the bucket in the grand scheme of things. They moved around, hunted, herded cattle, practiced horsemanship, and looked for suitable pastoral plains. Eventually, their focus tightened on the Mongolian Plateau, and they began to stick around. The Mongols were undoubtedly nomads, but that didn't mean they would move to a different land every week. Their nomadic lifestyle simply meant that they didn't focus much on agriculture and preferred to have the ability to pack up and leave when needed, and they usually did so when it was in their best interest.

Pre-Imperial Context

The time before the unification and the rise of the Mongols coincided with political rivalries, particularly between powerful Chinese dynasties. On top of that, the Chinese were in near constant conflict with the tribes to the north for centuries, particularly over land. The Chinese would often come into direct conflict with early Mongol tribes due to their expansion northward in search of farmland. This expansion forced the tribes to give up quality land and, in turn, they would often conduct raids on Chinese settlers.

From the 10th century onward, the Khitan Liao dynasty ruled a significant area of land in northern China and parts of Manchuria and eastern Mongolia. However, a federation of tribes known as the Jurchens grew stronger in northeastern China and founded the Jin dynasty. The Jurchens crushed the Liao dynasty in 1125 and seized much of their former territories. Taking over as the dominant authority in the area, the Jin dynasty soon came into conflict with the Mongol tribes as well, particularly the Khamag Mongols. The dynasty successfully resisted the Mongol onslaught, however.

Already at this point, the Khamag Mongol confederation emerged as something of a precursor for the latter Mongol state as we know it. The period of the 1130s also marks the first recorded Khan of the Mongols, known as Khabul Khan. Khabul was the Khan of the Khamag Mongols, but if we take this confederation as an early development of Mongol statehood, then he is the first Khan. In fact, Khabul Khan was the great-grandfather of Genghis Khan. Even though the wars against the Jin dynasty weren't very successful for the Khamag Mongols for a time, they undoubtedly became the dominant tribe on the Mongolian Plateau.

However, the early Mongols had two major problems. For one, their wars against the Jin were often wars of attrition and, as such, these conflicts weakened the already comparatively small Khamag Mongol confederation. Secondly, the Jin divide and conquer strategy among the nomadic tribes was still very successful, so the Mongols also had to fight against many tribes that were in a similar situation, notably the Tatars. Another competing power was west of Jin under the Tangut Western Xia Dynasty. To the south of Jin, the Chinese Song Empire was under the famous Song dynasty.

These and many other dynasties along with their respective states comprised much of what is now China and Kazakhstan. All the while, the Mongols, Tatars, Merkits, and other competing, nomadic tribes lay to the north of the main political landscape in the Asian heartland. Indeed, just like much of Asian history, the 12ᵗʰ century was a tumultuous time. The nomadic tribes fought each other, and the important dynasties struggled among themselves for supremacy. At the same time, the empire had to deal with the raiding nomads as well. This situation was a complex landscape of intertribal relations, however, and the different tribes and their confederations did occasionally come together to pursue common goals.

Toward the middle of the 12ᵗʰ century, the Jin dynasty and the Mongols reached an agreement after a Jin initiative to create peace. This time of peace allowed the Mongols to focus on settling their scores with other tribes, especially the Tatars. Prior to this, Mongol-Tatar relations turned sour after a Tatar betrayal that saw the Jin capture and execute Khabul Khan's successor. Therefore, the Tatars and the Mongols warred against each other well into the second half of the 12ᵗʰ century until a united offensive by the Tatars and the Jin inflicted a defeat on the Mongols in 1161.

Nonetheless, the early Mongols persevered and continued to attack, notably in 1205 when they struck against the Western Xia Empire, which would submit to the Mongols just a few short years later. A new day began for the Mongols as they now had one of the greatest war leaders at their helm. Genghis Khan was born just a year after the Tartars and Jin defeated the Mongols, and his life was quite a ride, unfolding throughout these early decades of the Mongol emergence.

Chapter II:
The Life and Rise of the
Great Khan

Genghis Khan - Mongolian Emperor

As you can see, the Mongols were strong people who were tempered by adversity and harsh life, but their potential was being squandered due to their disunity. The nearby regional powers were probably wary of these nomads since the start, which was why they did their best to keep the nomads bickering and fighting among themselves.

The nearby dynasties knew that if the Mongols were to unite, they would pose a major threat to their dominions. Soon the Mongols would realize their true power and unite to conquer the region, and all it took was one spark to set the process in motion.

Battle between Asian nomad tribes

That spark would come in the form of one special man, whose name would later become synonymous with the Mongols and their empire. That man was Genghis Khan. His successful rule and military conquests have been all but unparalleled in history. Genghis Khan has often been compared to other military leaders in history, such as Napoleon, Alexander the Great, and others, but few have conquered so much land and in such a short time. What's more, Genghis accomplished feats other great conquerors couldn't, such as the conquest of Russia.

Russia has been invaded many times by some of the most powerful armies in history, such as those of Napoleon and Hitler. And yet, neither Napoleon nor Hitler could subdue the Russians, both suffering immensely during the infamous Russian winter. The Mongols, on the other hand, would not be repelled. In fact, the icy winters in Russia often seemed to help the horse-mounted Mongols because they could easily storm across frozen rivers, which have otherwise always been significant natural barriers for armies throughout history.

Early Life

As with other aspects of Mongol history, most of what we know about Genghis' early life comes from outside sources, particularly from China and subsequent European explorers. Because of that, there are some minor disagreements on the facts, but we generally have a fairly accurate idea of the life of Genghis, especially once he rose to power.

Genghis Khan was born as Temujin most likely in 1162 to Yesugei, the leader of the Mongol Borjigin clan, and his wife, Hoelun. His place of birth is located in Burkhan Khaldun, a mountain in the Khentii Province of northeastern Mongolia. Mongol tradition suggests that baby Temujin was born with a blood clot in his fist, which is seen as a sign of destined greatness. Legends also tell us of Temujin's divine origins and his ancestor being a gray wolf. He was his father's eldest son, and the family wasn't very high up in the hierarchy. Temujin's father was a vassal of a more powerful tribal leader, and the family most likely had a tradition in blacksmithing.

The world that Temujin was born into was an unforgiving place that was hard on people in ways that we probably can't fathom nowadays. While Temujin was just a boy at around age nine, his father left him to live with the family of his future wife, according to a marriage arrangement. Like most Mongol boys, Temujin was expected to marry at the age of twelve, being a servant to the head of the family until that time. He also grew up with three brothers, two half-brothers, and a sister.

Not long after this arrangement, Temujin's father was killed by Tatars in an act of retaliation for their earlier conflicts. As the eldest son, Temujin was due to become the head of the Borjigin clan, but his young age discouraged support, and the family was soon abandoned. The rival Taychiut family used this opportunity to take over control of the entire clan. The following years were a time of great hardship for Temujin and his family who were now forced to live the nomadic lifestyle all by their lonesome, often struggling just to eat.

Temujin had to grow up quickly, so he practiced hunting, riding, and fighting, showing great promise. However, in his youth, Temujin showed his belligerent, ruthless side as well. Written legend has it that Temujin killed one of his half-brothers during a seemingly unimportant altercation. While this act was met with shock and great disapproval from his mother, it also consolidated Temujin as the head of his family.

Sometime later, most likely around 1182, Temujin spent some time in captivity and enslavement when the Taychiut captured him. By this time, Temujin already had ambitions, particularly within his former clan. Over time, he also attracted some supporters thanks to his charisma and adeptness at communication. He was also armed with valuable knowledge and lessons bestowed upon him by his mother, who taught him the value of alliances as a means of navigating the harsh political waters of tribal Mongolia.

As the story goes, Temujin's enslavement didn't last long. On the first night when he attempted to escape, he received help from one of the guards who saw him but, instead of apprehending him, decided to join Temujin's cause. Stories of

Temujin's life tell us of multiple such examples where Temujin's personality and drive impressed the people he met, motivating them to join him.

Ultimately, Temujin did marry his arranged wife, Borte of the tribe Konkirat, when he was around sixteen. However, bitter about Temujin's father's earlier transgressions against them, the Merkit tribe kidnapped Temujin's wife. In fact, Temujin's own mother, Hoelun, was a woman whom Yesugei had kidnapped from the Merkit before Temujin was born. Such was life in the Mongolian steppes during that time.

Temujin reacted quickly to the kidnapping of his wife. He elicited the help of the Keraites, whose Toghril Khan, also known as Ong Khan, had an oath of allegiance to Temujin's father. Toghril was a powerful man who wielded significant forces and political influence, and this allegiance changed Temujin's life forever. On top of helping Temujin recover his wife, Borte, Ong Khan also pledged to help Temujin reunite his former clan and take his rightful position as its leader. Ong Khan assembled thousands of men, and with the addition of the forces commanded by Temujin's childhood friend, Jamuka, they created a significant army.

Mongol army at rest

Needless to say, Temujin brought his wife back safe and mostly unharmed, and she gave birth to his firstborn son a few months later, naming him Jochi. Although Temujin would later have many wives, as per Mongol polygamous tradition at the time, Borte would serve as his empress. Temujin then made an "anda," or blood brother oath, with Jamuka just like his father and Ong Khan did before him. From this point onward, the race was on to subdue the other tribes and bring all the Mongols together under a single banner.

Mongol Unification

Of course, power sharing rarely works out, and there could be only one true Great Khan, so alliances became strained very quickly. For a while, this alliance was very strong and old rivals such as the Merkits would be crushed repeatedly in the ensuing wars. Temujin grew more powerful and influential each day thanks to his successes and his attractive personality.

Temujin's rise attracted negative attention fairly quickly, particularly from Ong Khan's son, Senggum, who began to plot an assassination against Temujin. Unfortunately, Ong Khan took his son's side and the relationship between him and Temujin grew colder. Temujin was well aware of the animosity and the plots, and he and Senggum would soon face off in open combat, where Temujin was repeatedly victorious.

To add insult to injury, Ong Khan later declined to marry one of his daughters to Temujin's son, Jochi, which was a major offense both to Mongol customs and to the alliance itself. A final split soon occurred between the two war leaders and Jamuka, Temujin's closest friend and confidant, chose Ong Khan's side. Once Temujin and his old friend parted ways, however, a significant portion of Jamuka's forces defected to Temujin.

Standing on his own, the future Genghis Khan was, by this point, already a warlord to be reckoned with. Even though Jamuka became estranged from Temujin and began to lean toward Ong Khan, the two didn't get along very well. Because of this and other factors, Temujin would ultimately crush Ong Khan and eventually destroy the Kerait tribe. All the while, Temujin was implementing a clever strategy wherein he would essentially buy people off with promises of great riches and spoils in the victories to come. Coupled with his successes and his charisma, many people agreed to submit, often without a fight.

Already by around 1190, Temujin had united most of the tribes that identified with the Mongol identity up to that point. This unification meant that he had a formidable and, most importantly, loyal force at his back. To feed and support this growing army, Temujin raided many surrounding tribes, inspiring terror far and wide. Many would simply surrender and pledge their allegiances while others had to be beaten into submission. Stories of Temujin's unstoppable war party spread quickly, reducing the number of potential challengers every day.

Genghis Khan at war

With the Keraites out of the way and a good part
of the Mongols consolidated behind him,
Temujin sought to bring more tribes under his

umbrella or destroy them. Another longtime rival was the tribe of Naimans, located to the west of the Mongols. Not only were the Naimans a threat beforehand but they now also had Jamuka on their side. Nonetheless, the indomitable Temujin crushed the Naimans as well as the Tatars in the end.

With each victory, Temujin made sure that he killed the nobility of the defeated tribes and anyone else who wielded political influence. These people, in his mind, were the carriers of old divisions and would surely be able to regroup their supporters at some point to instigate rebellions. After taking out such individuals, Temujin would incorporate all the soldiers and the common folk that he could into his Mongol tribes. Any old roots and ties to previous clan loyalties were cut, as Temujin was forging a new identity in the steppes – one that would bring all the nomads under a single banner and name.

However, in 1201, a Mongol political council, known as the Kurultai, was held with an undesirable outcome for Temujin. These gatherings were meetings of khans and other important tribal leaders, which served as a means of making certain decisions in Mongolia. The one in 1201 ended with Jamuka being proclaimed the Gur Khan, or "Universal Ruler," by the khans still loyal to him.

Temujin and Jamuka had been at odds for some time up to that point, but this proclamation drew the battle lines clearer than ever. A final showdown, which would determine the supreme leader of all the Mongols once and for all, was now imminent. Those tribal leaders who had paid attention to the unfolding events and could think ahead were quick to defect to Temujin's side. While Jamuka did form a sizeable coalition, Temujin's influence and popularity grew constantly.

Politically savvy people throughout the Mongolian Plateau were probably well aware of what was going on in the great scheme of things. It was becoming clearer that a great process of unification was afoot, and that only one man could emerge as the ruler of the steppes. Among those who switched camp to Temujin was Subutai, the brother of Jelme, a general who was one of Temujin's closest confidants.

The war would go on for a few years, and while Temujin did suffer some setbacks against Jamuka, he ultimately came out on top. Jamuka was betrayed and brought before Temujin as a captive around 1206. As legend has it, Temujin did offer a renewal of friendship to Jamuka, but the man refused it, acknowledging that there can be only one Great Khan and that Temujin had proved himself to be the greater man. He was given a noble death and the vast majority of his coalition submitted to Temujin. That same year, Temujin called a new Kurultai council and was finally proclaimed the Great Khan, taking the name and title of Genghis Khan.

Coronation of Genghis Khan

In all, Genghis Khan crushed the Merkits, Keraites, Tatars, Uyghurs, Naimans, and many other Mongol and Turkic tribes and confederations. Despite his ruthlessness, Genghis' charisma and leadership skills made him widely beloved, especially among the commoners he would integrate into his tribe. He also established a sort of meritocracy in that his inner circle men were appointed based on achievement and merit, not blood relations or name. And so, in 1206, Genghis Khan ascended as the sole great leader on the Mongolian Plateau, a renewed Mongol identity was forged from all the conquered and allied tribes, and the Mongol Empire was born.

Chapter III:
The Mongol Empire

Genghis Khan monument

What is born must also grow, of course, and so the period from 1206 onward was a time of glorious as well as brutal expansion for the Mongols. Before that, however, Genghis Khan focused on consolidating his realm, appointing all the right people to important positions, expanding his family, and building an even stronger army.

This period also shows us the intelligence and sophistication of Genghis Khan's state building, as told in the *Secret History of the Mongols*. This monumental piece of literature is the oldest preserved Mongol writing, which was created not long after Genghis passed away in 1227. This book is an invaluable piece of history of great importance to the Mongol nation and a major source for many things we know about the Mongols. *The Secret History* chronicles the life and exploits of Genghis Khan, but it also tells us much more about Mongol society in general.

The imperial stage of the Mongols lasted for a shorter time than other world's empires, but they managed to break the mold, innovate, and impress in many ways. Their cleverness, effectiveness, place of origin, and the speed with which they conquered half the world are all reasons why some people refer to the Mongols as one of history's greatest anomalies.

Consolidation

Sources vary, but most agree that Genghis Khan was most likely the ruler of around one to two-million people once his process of unification was finalized. Victory at war was only half the battle, however, as Genghis Khan now had to smash an entire system of undesirable traditions, outlooks, and values. The highly tribal and conflict-prone Mongolian Plateau could not change overnight just because one man won a bunch of battles.

Still, thanks to Genghis' example, everyone began to realize what could be accomplished if people gathered around a competent leader, set their petty conflicts aside, and stuck to their loyalties. The old system of tribes and clans was slowly but surely going extinct. The central ruler now had such a large following that those folks who still wanted to separate and run their own competing tribes simply found it wasn't worth their while anymore.

One of the innovations Genghis made was to extend his previous meritocratic ideas to most facets of society, not just his inner circle. Many aristocratic titles were abolished, and aristocrats who were suspected future rebels or trouble-makers were quickly removed to be replaced by competent men deemed right for the job. Most of the time under Genghis Khan, competence was valued over nepotism, which is the practice of favoring one's kin regardless of qualification. Furthermore, Genghis Khan outlawed the enslavement of other Mongols as well as the old practices of kidnapping and selling women. Theft of the most important Mongol resource – livestock – was now an offense that could yield the death penalty.

Perhaps more importantly, however, Genghis Khan soon ordered a writing system be introduced so that the predominantly illiterate

Mongols could begin to record information and educate themselves about the world. This decision shows us that Genghis thought ahead and that, to him, empire building was more than just land-grabbing. Genghis also instructed the empire's leadership to start conducting population censuses, and he introduced a system of diplomatic immunity for the ambassadors of foreign powers in Mongolia.

Ancient Mongolian parchment

During Genghis Khan's reign, the Mongols began their policy of religious tolerance toward the people they conquered. As long as they submitted to the new order, paid their tributes, and didn't cause trouble, newly incorporated populations were mostly left alone and allowed to maintain their cultural identity. This approach was incredibly progressive for that time, especially in contrast to places like Europe.

The vast majority of European countries were very stringently Christian and dogmatic. Putting aside the moral aspects of religious suppression, this mindset had other negative consequences in Europe. Dogmatism discouraged innovation and the emergence of new, useful ideas, which was one of the reasons why many important inventions in Europe made their way there from Asia, thanks to the Mongols.

Overall, Genghis Khan formed a sort of military and civil code that would govern Mongol politics and life for a long time to come. This system, called the Yassa code, was a unified code that would govern all the Mongol lands in an equal way. While its existence has been confirmed, the written code itself has never been found, so we only know those details that were outlined in other writings and oral traditions.

For instance, things like aristocracy, the upper echelons of society, weren't abolished, but both the aristocrats and the common folk were given clear roles in society, which meant both rights and obligations. The Yassa also listed other specific laws. The Mongol postal system, stretching far across the empire at all times and relying on messengers to quickly spread information and goods, was given special attention. The messengers employed in this service were protected, so disturbing or harming them in any way was a great crime.

Furthermore, while, as we mentioned, the Mongol social mobility and ranks were greatly based on merits, Genghis Khan's family was still enjoying a special status. His family enjoyed great riches thanks to the subsequent conquests, and Genghis expanded the family for a long time with many different wives, although his first wife, Borte, was the most important. He had four sons with her, and all of them were given regions to govern in the realm once they came of age. The highest authority in the country was certainly reserved for members of his Golden Family, as prescribed by Yassa.

Still, this was definitely the 13th century, and the Mongol conquests were undoubtedly often marked by brutality. Although they practiced their indigenous forms of shamanism, the Mongols weren't focused heavily on religion or race and ethnicity for that matter. Nonetheless, those who resisted in any way, such as Muslims in some regions, were utterly destroyed. The Mongols also used forced labor and threw many conquered folks into slavery, taking their women for themselves and desecrating entire civilizations.

These things almost never happened to those who chose to integrate peacefully, though.

Social engineering and politics aside, the Mongol society was still one built for war, focused primarily on the military. Genghis Khan used a decimal system to divvy up his forces into well-organized fighting units. Discipline and intense military training were crucial, and Genghis made sure that these standards were kept. On top of that, the military could never lack for anything – they had to be fed properly and well-equipped.

Mongolian war equipment

The real power of the Khan's army, however, was his ability to select the right people for the top slots in his army. Genghis Khan's top generals were usually either his sons or men who had proven themselves as staunch loyalists for years in the field. On top of all that, the generals were competent and judged by the Khan as qualified for the job. This combination of loyalty and skill ensured the cohesion and effectiveness of the army.

Genghis himself was a brilliant and, most importantly, adaptable military mind. His cavalry-based forces dominated the steppes, of course, but later on in his conquests, Genghis was up against tactics and military scenarios largely foreign to the Mongols. A particular issue was the people whom the Mongols would later fight were sedentary, living in fixed locations in walled-off cities. Genghis Khan's horse-mounted, steppe-prowling ways could not apply to besieging a city. Nonetheless, the Mongols quickly adapted and overcame these obstacles. Wherever the Khan would go, he would learn and immediately adopt something new. This flexibility ultimately led the Mongols to use catapults, siege construction, boiling hot oil, explosives, and many other things that enabled them to lay waste to cities.

With the competition neutralized and the newborn Mongol state firmly in place, Genghis

Khan could finally turn his attention to the ambitions beyond the borders. As legends tell us, Genghis Khan's dreams were constantly haunted by visions of great and glorious conquests in new, uncharted lands, especially those beyond the formidable walls built by the Chinese to keep the nomads such as him out. Genghis Khan felt it was time to pursue his true destiny, and the horde was ready.

Genghis Khan's Conquests

During much of Genghis Khan's rise to power, neighboring realms such as the Jin dynasty didn't pay much heed to the man. The Jin engaged in their usual politics and plots, trying to play the nomadic tribes against one another and probably underestimating Genghis Khan a great deal. In fact, during their wars with the Tatars, the Jin dynasty called upon Temujin to help them crush the constantly invading Tatars, which he did with great success.

As such, Genghis' military prowess was known far and wide sometime before he became the Great Khan in 1206. Nonetheless, the Jin dynasty still felt Genghis Khan would be largely inconsequential to their supremacy in the region. Indeed, Genghis Khan was very busy subduing the other nomadic tribes, and he really didn't pose a major threat to the Jin Empire for a while. Once he won and unified the Mongols, however, things would never be the same.

As Genghis Khan assumed his title in 1206, the hostilities with the Western Xia realm in northwestern China were already well underway. This major campaign would be the first Genghis Khan undertook outside the bounds of Mongolia. For the first few years, the conflict consisted largely of Mongol raids against the kingdom until 1209, when the Mongols fully committed to conquering them.

Genghis Khan's real goal from the start was China beyond the Great Wall, particularly the Jin dynasty to the south and east. However, the Western Xia was a threat that could strike from behind, so Genghis decided to neutralize them and secure his flank before new conquests. Genghis was also well-informed on the situation in both of these realms, knowing a young and inexperienced ruler headed the Jin dynasty at the time. This situation led Genghis to believe Jin wouldn't get involved if he attacked the Tangut Xia realm, and he was right.

Great Wall of China

Using newly adopted siege tactics, the Mongols quickly made their way to the gates of Yinchuan, the Xia capital. According to some sources, the Mongols even tried to divert a nearby river and flood the city instead of fighting, but this attempt failed. Nonetheless, the pressure caused by the thousands of battle-hardened Mongol horsemen was enough to force the Xia rulers to submit already in 1209.

This crushing victory propelled the Mongol horde to new heights. The Jin dynasty, however, quite foolishly decided to demand Genghis Khan's formal submission to their rule. As you have learned earlier, the Jin dynasty had a long history of meddling with Mongolian affairs, and they were effectively overlords of all the northern nomads for the most part. Things were changing irreversibly throughout the Mongolian Plateau and China, though, but the Jin dynasty didn't seem to get that memo.

Genghis decided he was ready in 1211, and he began to wage war against the Jin. During one of the first engagements, the ever-confident Jurchens sent a messenger, Ming-Tan, with demands to Genghis Khan's army instead of attacking first. The messenger quickly defected and gave away important information to Genghis, letting him know exactly where the Jin forces were waiting for them. What ensued was the Battle of Yehuling, or the Battle of Wild Fox Ridge, where the Jin army was utterly destroyed by September, although the Mongols suffered great casualties as well.

Over the next couple of years, Genghis Khan left a trail of destruction and desolation throughout the Jin borderlands. Jin cities deeper inside the country were forced to accept thousands of refugees, which put a great strain on their economies, leading to famine. Shortages of supplies forced the Jin armies to massacre many of their own people to contain the famine. The formerly subjugated Mongol nomads were wreaking havoc in the once mighty Jin realm, and the kingdom was in shambles.

Not even the Great Wall of China could keep the Mongols out, and they crossed the barrier in 1213, moving further into the country. After a string of victories, Genghis Khan laid siege to the Jin capital of Zhongdu (present-day Beijing) in 1214. Initially, the Jin emperor agreed to pay great tribute in silk, gold, silver, horses, and much more. The tribute was part of a submission agreement that subordinated the Jin to Genghis and guaranteed a cessation of hostilities. However, the Jin decided to move their capital to the south instead, which prompted a merciless reaction from Genghis. The Mongols quickly captured, sacked, and utterly destroyed Zhongdu shortly thereafter.

Genghis Khan soon began to spread out his campaigns across multiple fronts by sending his most competent and trusted generals in numerous directions. During the aforementioned campaign against the Jin dynasty, Genghis sent Jebe, or "the

Arrow," to subdue the remnants of the already defeated Naiman confederation, whose khan was now rebelling. The rebellious khan took over the Khanate of Kara-Khitan, which was friendly to Genghis. The competent general Jebe made short work of this task, and the Mongol empire incorporated Kara-Khitan. By 1218, Genghis Khan had expanded his realm all the way to Lake Balkhash in present-day eastern Kazakhstan. The Mongols now bordered Khwarazm, which was a Muslim empire stretching across present-day Turkmenistan, Afghanistan, Uzbekistan, and Iran.

Map including Lake Balkhash, Turkmenistan, Uzbekistan, and Kazakhstan

At this time, Genghis Khan didn't want to invade Khwarazm yet and instead sought to enter a trade agreement with them. The agreement was reached, but a local governor attacked and robbed the first trade caravan that arrived in Khwarazm, and its Muslim traders were massacred. These people were under Genghis Khan's protection, and so this attack was a sign of great disrespect and direct challenge. To add insult to injury, the Khwarazm ruler, Shah Ala ad-Din Muhammad II, denied Genghis compensation. On top of that, the diplomats Genghis then sent to negotiate were executed. Genghis Khan then mobilized his army, left his general, Muqali, in charge of pacifying the other rivals in China, and marched on Khwarazm.

Statues of two generals of Genghis Khan at the Government Palace

Khwarazm had brought upon itself the most destructive storm of Mongol fury, and the ensuing war was a spectacle of sheer brutality and destruction. Genghis stormed through the Islamic empire, pillaging, burning, and destroying cities one after another. Cities such a Samarkand, Urgench, and Bukhara were ravaged, with resisting soldiers, unskilled commoners, and aristocrats massacred or enslaved. In their usual fashion, the Mongols took in those folks whose skills they found useful, but the others were either killed or used as human shields.

By 1223, the Khwarazm lands were in ruins and littered with well over a million corpses. This war of terror was the ultimate testament to the Mongol reputation, and it cemented them as the most ferocious warring horde in the lands. Genghis Khan's dominion now stretched from the Sea of Japan to the Caspian Sea, virtually across all of Asia.

Chapter IV:
Genghis' Successors

Before Genghis Khan gathered his forces and left Khwarazm, he proclaimed his son Ogedei as his heir and successor. He devised a simple system of succession, which stated that all succeeding khans had to be his descendants. After that, the Mongol army was split in two, and Genghis led one part of it in raids throughout India and Afghanistan while Jebe and Subutai attacked locations in the Caucasus and present-day Russia. As usual, anyone who mounted any resistance was crushed, and the Mongols added Persia and Transoxiana to their empire. The entirety of the Mongol horde began to head home in 1225.

The Khan's Final Years

The Mongols came into hostile contact with numerous different peoples on their way back to Mongolia. After defeating the Georgians, other armies in Azerbaijan, and elsewhere around the Caspian Sea, a detachment led by Jebe and Subutai spent the winter near the Black Sea.

The Mongols later clashed with the forces of Kievan Rus, notably in the Battle of the Kalka

River in 1223. Other forces from the region supplemented the Kievan army, forming a coalition against the Mongols. It was to no avail, however, and the Mongols were victorious once again. Even though the Mongols then signed a peace deal with the Russians, the people of nobility were executed as usual.

One notable defeat the Mongols suffered during this time was at the hands of the Volga Bulgars, but soon the Mongols returned and crushed them on a second attempt, conquering Volga Bulgaria and laying down the foundation of what would later become the Golden Horde. In the end, the Mongols defeated everyone in their path and established their dominion around the entirety of the Caspian Sea.

Once Genghis Khan and his horde were back in Mongolia, Genghis set his sights on unfinished business in the neighborhood. While Genghis was campaigning in Khwarazm, the vassals in Western Xia refused to pledge their share of the forces to support the invasion, perhaps thinking that Genghis Khan would suffer a defeat against the Muslim forces. Not only that, but the Xia Tanguts joined forces with the remnants of the Jin dynasty and formed an alliance to defeat the Mongols.

Mongolian infantry warrior

This disobedience wasn't something that Genghis Khan could let go unpunished, so he focused on ending this resistance once and for all in one, final attack. The war began in 1226 and, during that year, Tangut cities and strongholds fell one after another. The Mongols attacked the Western Xia capital in 1227, promptly capturing it and pressing on until the last bits of resistance were extinguished. The Tanguts mounted a significant resistance and fought hard, but they were no match for the battle-hardened, overwhelming Mongol horde. The Western Xia Empire surrendered that same year, which brought an end to their 189 years of dominion. Seeing no value in keeping around the aristocracy that betrayed him many times, Genghis Khan slaughtered the ruling dynasty.

Genghis was well aware of two important things. First and foremost, he knew an empire as vast as his could not last under just one ruler and without any kind of decentralization. Secondly, like all intelligent war leaders, he knew any day could be his last. Because of these concerns, Genghis divided up his empire into a few khanates that would be ruled by regional rulers made up of his sons and grandsons. These rulers were supposed to be subordinate to the Great Khan, Genghis' own direct successor, Ogedei Khan. This idea later led to the formation of different Mongol khanates, some of which would continue to rule their regions for centuries after Genghis Khan.

Genghis Khan died during the last days of Xia resistance, on August 18, 1227. The death of such a glorious leader was a monumental event, so it spawned quite a bit of folklore and legend. Because of this, history isn't certain on the details of Genghis' death. A common account is the one where he fell off a horse due to fatigue, suffering an internal injury. He is said to have continued to lead his army but ultimately succumbed to his injury and died in his sleep.

As per the Great Khan's request, he was buried in an unmarked grave that has never been found. As in life, legends surrounded Genghis in death as well. Mongol folklore talks about the burial in great detail. Folks said that the mighty funeral party, consisting of fierce warriors most loyal to the Great Khan, killed all witnesses to the funeral.

Genghis Khan mausoleum near Ordos, Inner Mongolia, China

Troubled Successions

Genghis Khan was survived by many children and a massive, elite army. The Mongol cavalry and other forces had come a long way since Genghis' humble beginnings. This army was no rugged band of raiders anymore; Genghis' cavalry was elite, well-equipped, well-trained, highly experienced, and battle-hardened. These horsemen constituted a great chunk of the total army, which, at the time of Genghis' death, numbered close to 130,000 men. These forces were shared and assigned to the command of the Great Khan's sons, grandsons, and other relatives.

Genghis' successor, Ogedei Khan, was a successful ruler who reigned between 1229 and 1241. He established his seat of power at Karakorum in central Mongolia, which would serve as the capital between 1235 and 1260. Incredibly enough, the Mongol conquests not only continued but intensified during this time. Some historians believe the Mongols became even more ferocious after the death of their first Great Khan. By the time the Mongols finished off Western Xia later in 1227, this civilization was all but exterminated.

Under Ogedei, the Mongols seized lands deep inside Persia, crushed the last remaining

Khwarazmids, and finally came into contact with the Chinese Song dynasty in the southeast. Of course, this contact was very quickly marked by hostilities, and it was the beginning of a prolonged period of warfare between the two powers, which would last all the way until 1279.

In the late 1230s, the Mongols focused even more on invading the farther reaches of Russia and Europe. These attacks were led by Batu Khan, the ruler of the Blue Horde, one of the sub-regions, as envisioned by Genghis Khan. The Mongols thus carved a path into Central Europe as well. By 1241, Batu Khan and general Subutai were fighting Poles, Germans, and Hungarians, creating vassals almost everywhere they went. These Mongol forces stopped at Vienna and return to Mongolia in 1241 when news broke that Ogedei Khan had died.

What ensued was a troubled period and a succession crisis, where Ogedei's widow ruled over the empire as a regent for five years. There were rivalries between many of Genghis' grandsons and the integrity of the empire began to waver. After this five-year regency, Ogedei's widow managed to appoint her son, Guyuk Khan as the ruler. However, Guyuk's tenure as the Great Khan was short-lived and sometimes challenged, particularly by Batu Khan, who refused to acknowledge his authority. Guyuk died in 1248, paving the way for another three years of regency and instability.

A degree of stability returned to the Mongol Empire with the ascension of Mongke Khan, who ruled until 1259. The Mongol Empire was becoming an even more interesting place by this time, being influenced by all the cultures they came into contact with. European accounts from the capital Karakorum in 1254 spoke of churches, mosques, and Buddhist temples being built one next to another.

By most accounts, Mongke was a good and kind ruler to his people, but he too managed to expand the empire further with the help of his two brothers, Hulegu and Kublai. During this time, the Mongols conquered great portions of present-day Iran and Iraq and sacked the city of Baghdad in 1258, which served as the capital of the mighty Abbasid Caliphate during that time.

Hulegu Khan mobilized his forces for conquest in present-day Syria in 1259. The initial attacks were successful as usual, and the Mongols had now reached the Mediterranean, preparing to strike southward into Palestine and then Egypt, with the ultimate goal being the domination of North Africa. However, the Mongols finally met their match when they clashed with Egyptian Mamluks, many of whom were enslaved Slavs with valuable experience in fighting the Mongols earlier. On top of that, the bulk of the Mongol forces had already withdrawn back to Mongolia after news of Mongke Khan's death in 1259. The Mongols were defeated at the Battle of Ayn Jalut in 1260 and, for the first time in history, didn't return with a vengeance.

A statue of Kublai Khan at a government palace

Already in 1260, Kublai had secured his spot as the next Great Khan via a vote while he was campaigning in China, although the succession was challenged once again. The main competing claimant was Arigboge, Kublai's younger brother in the capital Karakorum. Hulegu, who was at that time still campaigning in Syria, would later come into conflict with Kublai and Hulegu's cousin, Berke.

While Kublai was mostly recognized as the Great Khan, fractures began to show throughout the empire. The state was perhaps too vast and diverse to control for long. Nonetheless, the period roughly between 1250 and 1350 would come to be known as the Century of Peace, or Pax Mongolica. The Mongol conquests brought about a relative peace in the grand scheme of things and a connection between the eastern and western worlds, facilitating trade like never before.

Chapter V:
The Final Decades of Unity and Decline

As we mentioned earlier, Genghis' will was for the empire to be split up into subregions subordinate to the central authority of the Great Khan. From a political standpoint, this move was necessary, but then again, it also meant that the lines for separation and disintegration were set. The main khanates to emerge were the Blue and White Horde khanates, which later became the Golden Horde under Batu Khan, Il-Khanate (Hulegu), Empire of the Great Khan in China (Kublai), Mongol heartland with Karakorum (Tolui), and Chagatai Khanate, ruled by Chagatai.

Street view of the city and the gate of the Palace of the Khan of the capital city of Golden Horde Sarai-Batu

The vast empire was divided between a few very powerful people and their successors. The different khanates were mostly under the rule of Genghis Khan's sons, grandsons, and relatives, but rivalries would emerge nonetheless.

Kublai Khan

Despite the emerging issues, Kublai Khan was undoubtedly one of the greatest Mongol leaders, as well as the last Great Khan to be universally recognized. Because of his dispute with his brother, Arigboge, Kublai established his own capital in Khanbaliq, present-day Beijing. Kublai made this move in 1260 and would initiate reconstruction projects in the city during 1267. Here, Kublai would begin to identify more and more with being a Chinese emperor.

It would seem this immersion was something of a trend throughout the Mongol Empire during Kublai Khan's rule. Namely, regional khans, and with them their followers, began to absorb more influence from the vastly diverse people the Mongols conquered. Some converted from Mongol shamanism and other traditional religious practices to Islam, Christianity, Buddhism, and the like. This factor was perhaps one that contributed to the eventual fragmentation of the empire.

Kublai Khan hunting, transported in a palanquin carried by four caparisoned elephants

Between 1260 and 1264, Kublai managed to defeat his younger brother in battle during a war of succession known as the Toluid Civil War, named after the Tolui family, which both the brothers belonged to. Ten years and many successful conquests later, Kublai Khan was the first Great Khan who attempted to invade the Japanese archipelago. Japan was a tough nut to crack, however, thanks to its isolation. Despite hundreds upon hundreds of ships, the invasion failed because the armada was struck by typhoons.

Japanese Warriors Repel Mongol Invasion

In 1279, Kublai was able to finally crush the last remnants of the Chinese Song dynasty after more than forty years of warfare started by Ogedei Khan. He established the Yuan dynasty some years before that, which was essentially Mongol rule in China. This move gave birth to a Mongol-Chinese empire that would last well into the 14th century. Even as such, Kublai Khan is remembered as one of the greatest rulers in the long Chinese history.

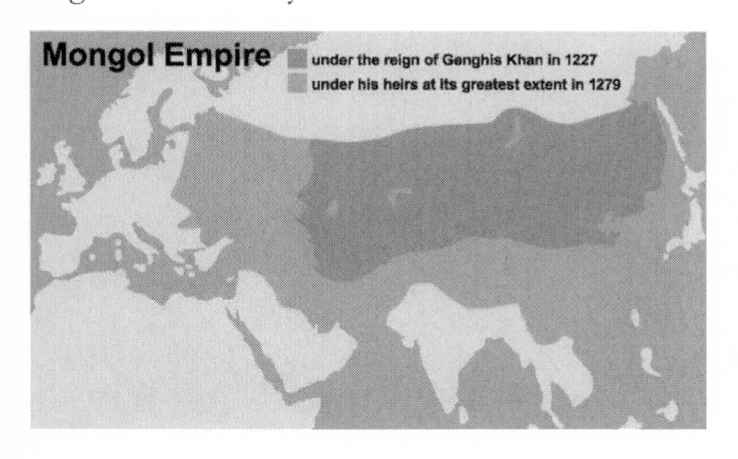

Mongol Empire Genghis Khan

Kublai strayed further and further from his Mongol identity, however, which drew a wedge between his realm and the western khanates.

Kublai's culture essentially became Chinese over time. What's more, once he defeated and conquered the Song Empire, Kublai didn't initiate the typical slaughter of aristocracy. He sought to have them under his control, probably as a means of giving legitimacy to his rule over the native Chinese folk. He also ensured that, once the fighting was done, his army didn't pillage and plunder.

Nonetheless, Kublai did initiate certain discriminatory measures against the Han Chinese nobility, stripping them of titles and riches when he saw fit. China had other ethnic groups as well, which Kublai promoted and favored over the Han Chinese. Despite being a foreign conqueror, Kublai revitalized and improved China in many ways, particularly in the areas of economy and infrastructure. During the 1270s, the famous European explorer, Marco Polo, visited these lands. He brought back stories of incredibly advanced culture and civilization, both in regards to old China and the Mongol rule. In fact, Marco Polo's tales were so incredible that many in Europe labeled him a fraud, only to later learn that everything he said was the truth.

Bust statue of Marco Polo, in Villa Borghese Park, Rome

In addition to Japan, Kublai also tried and failed to conquer Dali in present-day southwestern China and Vietnam. In 1281, Kublai tried once again to invade Japan with hundreds of ships and tens of thousands of men. The Mongols engaged in some bitter fighting with Japanese Samurai warriors, but, incredibly enough, the Mongols were once again beset by treacherous weather, ultimately failing to conquer Japan.

Kublai Khan's attempted invasion of Japan in 1281

Kublai Khan died in 1294. He managed to accomplish quite a lot, most notably a firm and secure Mongol hold on the entirety of China. He was the last true Great Khan and remains one of the greatest Mongol rulers, even though some aspects of his reign probably contributed to the eventual total disintegration of the realm. Kublai Khan's rule was the last time the old Mongol Empire would function as a whole. After his death, four distinct khanates were consolidated: the Golden Horde, Il-Khanate, Chagatai Khanate, and the Yuan Dynasty.

Over time, these khanates would drift further and further apart, each wanting to pursue its own destiny, often with little regard to the customs of Genghis Khan's Mongol Empire.

Disintegration

With the disintegration of the Mongol Empire well underway and growing schisms between the interests of the mostly independent khanates, keeping the Silk Road open became more difficult. This historically crucial trading route between the East and the West was kept alive thanks to the security guarantees provided by the Mongol Empire, so the period was referred to as Pax Mongolica, or Mongol Peace. Despite all the constant conquests and warfare, the one thing that could be counted on by all of Eurasia was the Silk Road. With the death of Kublai, however, the Silk Road's future seemed grim.

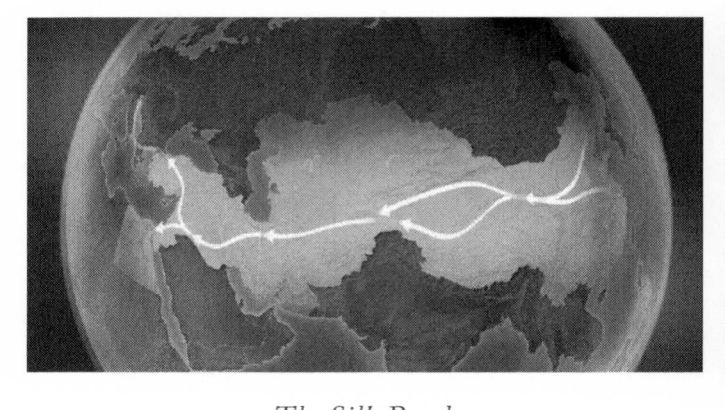

The Silk Road

Kublai Khan's rule over in the Yuan Dynasty was succeeded by his grandson, Temur, who ruled between 1295 and 1307. He wasn't the Great Khan, however, as the position was all but abolished in practice. Temur had to maintain Mongol rule over China but also deal with attacks from other Mongols, particularly those from Genghis Khan's lineage. He successfully defended the realm from these attacks and from domestic rivals, though, so his rule was very successful.

Successions throughout the Mongolian and Chinese parts of the empire became increasingly chaotic into the 14th century. During all this time, Kublai's cousins, Batu and Berke, in the Golden

Horde and his brother, Hulegu, in Persia grew stronger and more independent. Even though its authority over the western khanates dwindled, the Yuan Dynasty would persist until 1368 on its home grounds. The last Great Khan, even if in name only, was Toghon Temur, and he ruled between 1333 and 1368. Toghon Temur acquired this title when he was only thirteen and history has recorded him as an overall weak and ineffective ruler.

Until Toghon came of age, control over the empire was given to the regency of Bayan, even though his policies were often very detrimental to the Chinese. Native Chinese elites had already been growing their hatreds for a long time, but this period deepened the divide. Chinese nobility grew increasingly weary of the Mongols. Toghon Temur's rule as khan came to an end in 1368 when a rebelling Chinese ex-monk, Zhu Chongba, drove the Mongol ruler out of Beijing. This end was the birth of the famous Chinese dynasty called Ming, and the Mongol hold over China was thus brought to an end. Official history holds 1368 as the year when the Mongol Empire officially ended.

In the coming years, the Ming still fought many wars against the Mongols. The Mongols formed the Northern Yuan Dynasty to continue the struggle, but that one was also crushed around

1382. During this time, the Chinese assimilated all of the Mongol nobles who remained in the country, which meant they had to change their names and customs to fully integrate into the Chinese identity. China also purged the foreign religions from their land, particularly Christianity and, to a great extent, Islam. From this point on, the relationship between China and the Mongols on the Mongolian Plateau mostly reverted back to what it was during the times of the Jin. The Chinese formed a frontier toward the nomads and tried, albeit unsuccessfully, to conquer all of Mongolia.

Elsewhere in Eurasia, however, the other legacy empires continued to exist, some longer than others. The Il-Khanate in Persia, for instance, had been developing along a different path while all of this was happening in China. The Khan of this realm converted to Islam in the late 13th century, changing the whole orientation of the khanate. This country had very little to do with the original Mongol Empire, and their Mongol identity was simply dissolved by the 15th century. The khanate was conquered by Timur along with most of Persia in 1383.

In Central Asia and Russia, the Golden Horde officially persisted until the early 16th century, but its influence diminished all the time. Unified in a desire to rid themselves of Mongol rule, the local

Russian and other Slavic nobles eventually gained their independence. The Chagatai Khanate, which was located across present-day eastern Kazakhstan and a number of other countries in the region, was split into eastern and western portions during the 14th century, and the eastern portion lasted until the latter 17th century, although drastically changed and much more Turkic than Mongol.

Even though it fell apart in fewer than two centuries, the Mongol Empire impacted the world on an unprecedented scale. The legacy of Genghis Khan continues to impress, and its signs are everywhere. Genetic studies have shown that 1 in roughly 200 men today carry Genghis Khan's genes. What's more, this mere herder from the steppes made himself the great leader of dissociated nomadic tribes and created an entire nation, which still exists. There are between 10 and 11 million Mongols living on the Mongolian Plateau to this day, carrying and keeping alive the legacy of their Great Khan and once unstoppable empire.

Chapter VI:
Legacy and Impact

As you have seen throughout our examination of all this important history, there was a lot of warfare and conquest. However, throughout our chronicles about the Mongols, you were also able to see the other aspects of their empire and of the Mongols as a people. As such, the Mongols have made quite a legacy for themselves and they have been pioneers in many fields. In this chapter, we will take a quick look at a few more important inventions, contributions, achievements, and the ways in which the Mongols have affected our world.

Trade

The period of relative stability and peace during the Pax Mongolica meant a lot more than just a cessation of total warfare. This stability facilitated trade and, thanks to the sheer vastness of the Mongol Empire, distant regions were connected and able to transfer all sorts of goods from one end to the other. The Silk Road provided a venue for commerce between China and Europe. These two regions were very different, and Europe had much to gain from the advanced civilization in China.

People used the Silk Road to share much more than just raw goods. The flow of ideas was just as, if not more important than material resources. Not only were these regions connected, but the trading routes were also kept very safe and secure, especially by medieval standards. According to popular wisdom at the time, one could traverse the Mongol Empire on foot, carrying a golden plate on his head, without worrying for his safety. The security and prosperity of the trading routes was important for the Mongols because it was a source of taxes.

Spread of Technology

As usual, with the exchange of culture and ideas comes a technological exchange. As the famous explorer Marco Polo noted in the 13th century, many regions in Asia, especially China, were populated by highly advanced civilizations for their time. In fact, many of the things he wrote about and reported back in Europe were met with great skepticism.

Thanks to the Silk Road, however, a lot of the things he talked about made their way to Europe for all to see. Among these things, there were

75

numerous important technological breakthroughs achieved in China, which Europe would later heavily rely upon. Among these innovations were gunpowder, advanced paper making, and many other things that we now take as normal. While the Mongols themselves didn't exactly invent many of the things that Europe got thanks to the Silk Road, they undoubtedly made it possible for these crucial exchanges to take place. In fact, in many instances, these exchanges altered the course of human history.

Science and Globalization

Overall, the majority of inventions and scientific breakthroughs that the Europeans adopted from China made their way there via the Silk Road. In a way, making these transfers possible was just as important as the invention of this technology. New scientific breakthroughs wouldn't have been of much use to the world if they were limited to isolated societies in East Asia.

However, the Mongols didn't just build the Silk Road and go about their way. Instead, they made sure they got much more from this trade than just taxes. Because of the vastness of their empire, the Mongols had access to knowledge from distant parts of the world such as India, Persia, and the Middle East. All of these regions were home to great civilizations that had much to offer. Particularly important was the transfer of medical innovation and knowledge, and the Mongols dedicated themselves to studying Western medicine in depth, particularly under Kublai Khan.

This system of far-reaching trade and back and forth exchange was really an early form of free trade and globalization. These things are now an integral part of the human experience with many free trade agreements and economic unions, but it was the Mongol Empire and its Silk Road that pioneered the idea.

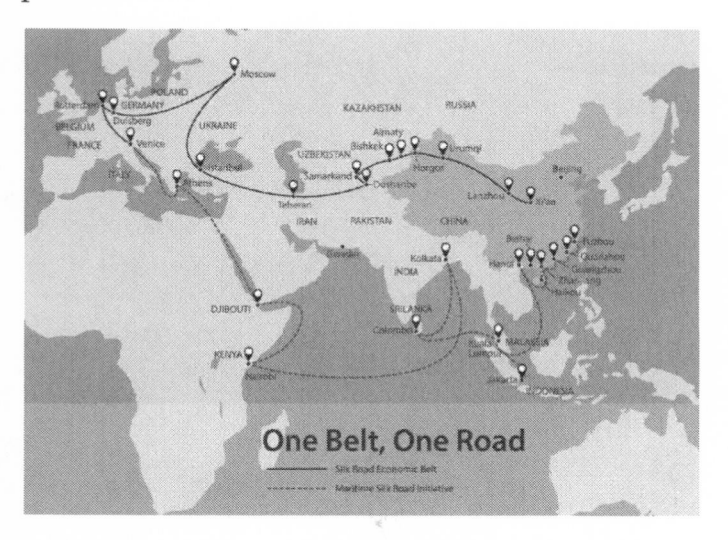

One Belt, One Road, Chinese strategic investment in the 21st century map

Spread of Firearms

The Mongols were quick to adopt many Chinese inventions that proved crucial in warfare, particularly gunpowder. One of the most prominent weapons that the Mongols used was the contemporary equivalent of grenades. These explosive devices struck fear into the enemy and made the Mongols a force to be reckoned with, especially during sieges.

Over time, such tactics made their way to Europe, and the Europeans were quick to pick up on the potential of gunpowder. Of course, this tactic had a major impact on the subsequent development of firearms, which brought an end to the days of knighthood and ushered in a whole new era in warfare. Eventually, the Europeans would conquer the world thanks to firearms, often subduing entire civilizations in the New World with little more than a few hundred men at arms. Over time, the innovations in this weaponry brought about the emergence of things like artillery and changed the concept of war forever.

Russia

As students of history know, Russia is still an indomitable country that has never been successfully conquered, except once. Indeed, the early days of Russian statehood saw many invasions and conquests by the Mongols who eventually held most of Russia in subjugation.

Ironically, some historians argue the Mongolian conquests led to the formation of Russia that we know today. The numerous Russian states at the time, such as Kievan Rus, Moscow, and others, were eventually forced to unite in order to push back and force the Mongols out of their lands. Separated by political leadership, language connected the Russian people, and in 1480, they managed to unite and defeat the Golden Horde. Eventually, the Russians would push further into Mongol-held areas, expanding their territories and finally building their own empire in the 18th century.

Other Military Inventions

Mongolian nomad

As you have learned, the Mongols were big on horse archery and, as such, they made some very important contributions and improvements to this art of war. One example was the Mongolian composite bow, which was vastly superior to the bows used in many other regions. As opposed to traditional, single-piece bows, composite bows were complex devices comprised of parts. Mongolian bows were vastly superior when it came to range, accuracy, and sheer power. They used horns, wood, sinew, and other materials to make their bows very durable and effective.

The Mongols also vastly improved one crucial aspect of horsemanship: the stirrup. As you may or may not know already, stirrups are footrests that greatly improve a rider's ability to control their horse and remain securely in the saddle. The stirrup has been around for a while, but the Mongols might have been the first people to use highly advanced metal stirrups over eleven centuries ago. The Mongols were able to stay glued to their horses in the heat of battle no matter what, often riding at great speeds and engaging enemies with their bows at the same time.

Riding stirrup

Dried Milk

Being a highly mobile, nomadic military force, the Mongols had to rely on durable and highly portable sources of nutrition that could keep them going in the field. One such innovation was dried milk, a quite common and accessible product nowadays.

Namely, the Mongols figured out that they could use the leftover curds after processing their milk into butter and cheese instead of just throwing it away. The Mongols would then dry out these bits and pieces, usually in the sun, and grind them down into powder. This primitive powder milk could be stored for cold winter months or taken on expeditions. All that the Mongols had to do was bring the milk back into liquid form with a bit of warm water. Of course, this potion was far from fresh milk, but it provided sustenance and, above all, convenience.

Support for Art

Being a warlike people that preferred the nomadic lifestyle well into their imperial stage, the Mongols weren't big on writing or producing fine art. In an interesting twist, however, they were admirers who had respect for art. Even though those who resisted their rule were squashed mercilessly, the

Mongols would allow and support the artistic expression of the people they came in contact with.

During peaceful times, the Mongols were sort of like patrons for those local artists who impressed them. The Mongols thus protected and encouraged the art they liked under most of the Khans. Seeing as their empire stretched so far and wide, the Mongols came into contact with all sorts of artists in the Middle East, parts of India, elsewhere in Asia, and other locales. Over time, they also started to commission those artists to bring the Mongols' own designs to life in architecture, stonework, textile, and other fine crafts. In a way, the Mongols outsourced these jobs to those whom they perceived as skilled.

Postal System

An empire as vast as that of the Mongols needs a way for information to flow quickly and efficiently, and the Mongols were well aware of this. This was why they built something called the Yam route. The Yam was essentially a messenger system or a primitive form of postal service, and it stretched across important Mongolian lands.

Genghis Khan was the first to pay special attention to this system, expanding it to new lengths and making it perhaps the most efficient such system in the world. The Yam was basically a string of relay stations and resting stops that provided shelter, vital supplies, horses, and other necessities for messengers. The system was constantly buzzing with activity and it provided the intelligence backbone of the Mongol armies. Well-trained messengers could cover more than 150 miles each day using the Yam. Being such an important system, the Yam was maintained by the Russians well after the Mongols were forced out of their lands.

Progressive Outlook

As much as they loved to conquer places, the Mongols weren't particularly obsessed with things like ideologies and religion. Certainly, the Mongols had their shamanist customs and rituals, but it wasn't the most important thing in the world, especially when it came to imposing Mongolian rule on conquered peoples. As such, the Mongols generally practiced a policy of tolerance, and the indigenous, conquered folks were left to practice whatever religion they pleased. In fact, the local religious leaders under Mongolian rule were often spared from paying taxes.

Overall, as long as they submitted to the will of the Mongols and paid their tributes, the conquered peoples in the Mongol Empire enjoyed a degree of autonomy. The Mongols cultivated the beliefs, skills, ideas, and knowledge of the cultures they incorporated into the empire, making them a very progressive force at the time, perhaps in stark contrast to their otherwise warlike ways.

Conclusion

It is entirely possible that, prior to reading this book, your perception of the Mongols was that of a tribe that did little more than pillage, loot, and raid the lands of Asia. Any such misconceptions should be dismantled now that you have learned the broader story of the Mongols and their empire.

Certainly, warfare and destruction are an important part of Mongolian history and legacy, but, truth be told, these things are a legacy of the world itself. War and conquest permeate all of human history, and the Mongols just happened to have been extraordinarily adept at such things.

Much more importantly, the Mongolian Empire was a state built by folks who knew how to keep up with the times. The Mongols put to use many ideas and technologies of the day and were very much capable of making these things work for them. On top of that, the Mongols were innovative and creative in everything they did beyond just warfare.

The story of the Mongol Empire is also a great testament to how empires rise and fall, exemplifying a process that has been part of the human experience for millennia. Sometimes, the process is more gradual and, in other cases, it occurs overnight in historical terms, but the pendulum always keeps swinging.

All in all, even though the Mongol Empire was relatively short-lived, it impacted this world considerably more than some of the civilizations that had existed for a much longer time. And as you have learned, a lot of that impact was greatly beneficial and positive for the world.

More from Us

Made in the USA
Middletown, DE
22 November 2022